MAKING WAR &
MAKING PEACE

PEACE·AND·JUSTICE·SERIES 8

MAKING WAR & MAKING PEACE

Why Some Christians Fight and Some Don't

DENNIS BYLER

HERALD PRESS
Scottdale, Pennsylvania
Kitchener, Ontario

Library of Congress Cataloging-in-Publication Data
Byler, Dennis, 1949-
    Making war and making peace : why some Christians fight and
some don't / Dennis Byler.
        p.   cm. — (peace and justice series ; 8)
    Bibliography: p.
    ISBN 0-8361-3497-4
    1. War—Religious aspects—Christianity. 2. Peace— Religious
aspects—Christianity. 3. Just war doctrine. I. Title. II. Series
BT736.2.B95   1989
241'.6242—dc20   89-2222
                                                                            CIP

∞™

The paper used in this publication meets the minimum requirements of
American National Standard for Information Sciences—Permanence of
Paper for Printed Library Materials, ANSI Z39.48-1984.

MAKING WAR AND MAKING PEACE
Copyright © 1989 by Herald Press, Scottdale, Pa. 15683
    Published simultaneously in Canada by Herald Press,
    Kitchener, Ont. N2G 4M5. All rights reserved.
Library of Congress Catalog Number: 89-2222
International Standard Book Number: 0-8361-3497-4
Printed in the United States of America
Cover sculpture by Esther K. Augsburger;
    photograph by Jan Gleysteen
Design by Gwen M. Stamm

1 2 3 4 5 6 7 8 9 10 96 95 94 93 92 91 90 89

To Mateo, my son

Contents

Foreword

History shows that during the first centuries of the Christian church, Christians did not go to war. They were committed to settling differences peacefully. Their opposition to warfare was based on the life and teachings of Jesus.

This stance began to change around the beginning of the fourth century. Emperor Constantine's edict of toleration in A.D. 313 marked the beginning of a new era. From then on, Christians began to serve actively in the military in obedience to the state.

In this brief book, the author discusses how and why most Christians came to accept participation in warfare. He uses illustrations, quotes, stories, and dialogue to show how all Christians were eventually expected to join the state in fighting national enemies. Later on, Christians moved into political leadership and began taking responsibility for government policies and actions, such as fighting in wars.

The author draws from the Scriptures and from history to show another way to resolve conflicts. He calls for turning our backs on this Christendom arrangement and for identifying the real enemy—the dark spiritual forces of the universe.

Will we fight the enemy with the spiritual weapons of Ephesians 6, with the full armor of God? he asks. Or will we go on killing people as if they were the real enemy?

He shows how pagan, Greek, and Roman influences shaped Christian thought and action about warfare. Does Jesus' way of nonviolent love really make a difference? he asks. Is love for national enemies really possible?

Making War and Making Peace is number eight in a series on peace and justice themes listed inside the back cover. It is a sequel to book number two which traces the theme from the time of the early church until Constantine. For further reading on the theme of this book, check the references near the end.

—*J. Allen Brubaker, Editor*
Peace and Justice Series

Introduction

When I was requested to write this book, the editors explained their plan for a series of books that would translate well into many national situations. They didn't want a book centered on the United States' experience, for example.

The more I think about the matter, the more I am convinced that an international perspective is the most appropriate for it. Part of what has gone wrong with Christian thinking about war is that the church has been drawn into national divisions. That was not God's original intention. Paul's letters vibrate with the joy of discovering that the new reality in Jesus Christ unites people of the most diverse nationalities and cultures. The new kingdom, of which Jesus is Lord, breaks down the long-standing enmity between citizens of every other nation.

In 1982, Argentina and Britain fought a war over the Falkland/Malvinas Islands. Shortly thereafter, I, who was born in Argentina, had the privilege of hosting two Englishmen in our home in Spain. As we talked, I realized something that made me chuckle. In our conversation, they were using the Argentine name for the islands, the Malvinas, and I was using the British name, the Falklands. Without intending to, we had discovered that it is possible to move beyond national pride. In those months in 1983, a couple of the most moving experiences for me were to hug English and Scottish Christians. Even war between our two countries could not break the unity we had found in Jesus Christ.

At the time, the clergy of both countries were routinely claiming the war met all the requirements of justifiable war. Christians of both countries were glad to kill each other with the blessing of their priests and pastors.

There has to be a better way.

—Dennis Byler
Burgos, Spain

PART ONE

The Fourth-Century Watershed

CHAPTER 1

How Many Attitudes Toward War Can Be Christian?

Why do some Christians fight and some don't? You may be asking yourself, why is there a difference of opinion on this?

Didn't Jesus Christ settle the issue himself? Isn't the New Testament clear about it? Well, many Christians think so. Still, in 2,000 years we Christians have managed to disagree over just about everything. It should come as no surprise that we don't all think the same on this matter today either.

And yet, the point is a good one. Did Jesus address the issue? Because if Christ himself took a position concerning how to deal with our enemies, then only that should be labeled the truly Christian position. The rest would simply be non-Christian positions, even if certain Christians hold them. As a matter of fact, there really is a Christian position on war in just that sense. Jesus did talk about how to deal with enemies. He said *to love them.*

To what?

Love them.

Obviously, Christians are to be patient and forgiving and all that. It just wouldn't do for you to hate your mother-in-law or your sister. Not even your neighbor when his barking dog keeps you awake at night. But did Jesus mean for us to love wartime enemies?

Christians have had many different opinions about war. So many we will not be able to deal with all of them. John H. Yoder is a well-known Christian professor at Notre Dame University in the United States. In his book *Nevertheless*, he identified 16 different varieties of Christian "pacifism." Now Christian pacifists are fairly rare to begin with, so just imagine how much variety there must be among the rest! Still, the various approaches usually fit into certain patterns. In this book, we will identify and describe those patterns.

The Source of Most Christian Thinking on War

Have you ever heard a Christian and non-Christian argue about war? If not, you may be surprised to learn that most Christian thinking about war follows pagan philosophy.

Plato was a Greek philosopher who lived more than 300 years before Christ. He wrote that war should be fought in such a way as to make reconciliation possible and further wars unnecessary. The purpose of peace is not just to mark time till the next war.

Rather, war itself is the undesirable situation. Peace is the true objective.

Cicero, a Latin writer who died a few years before Jesus was born, had this to say about war:

> There are certain duties that we owe even to those who have wronged us. For there is a limit to retribution and to punishment; or rather, I am inclined to think, it is sufficient that the aggressor should be brought to repent of his wrongdoing, in order that he may not repeat the offense and that others may be deterred from doing wrong. . . . The only excuse, therefore, for going to war is that we may live in peace unharmed; and when the victory is won, we should spare those who have not been blood-thirsty and barbarous in their warfare.[1]

Most Christians even today would probably feel pretty comfortable with these principles. If anything, we may be surprised to discover that its writer was a pagan living before Christ. It sounds so right; so sober, peace-loving, balanced, so Christian.

Which is just the point. The way most Christians approach the matter of war is not especially unique. At least, not unique in the startling way that Jesus was unique when he said, "Love your enemies."

As a matter of fact, Christians for the first three centuries did not go to war. As you read Christian writers of that period you notice them insisting that Christianity is not a religion for shirkers and traitors. They said, "We are not interested in profiting from the sacrifice of others. We believe *prayer* is the real way to peace. And we are not traitors. We wouldn't fight for the enemy either!"

Back then there really was a truly Christian attitude about war. A uniquely Christian attitude, which differed from even Plato or Cicero. An attitude which could only be traced back to Jesus himself. (In another book in this series, *How Christians Made Peace with War*, author John Driver describes the original Christian teaching on war.) But things just did not stay the way Jesus lived and taught.

The Emperor Who Changed His Clothes

You may know the story by Hans Christian Andersen about the emperor's new clothes. Certain rascals showed up at the palace claiming they could weave magical cloth from gold. Only the people who deserved their jobs could see it, they said. For everyone else, the cloth would be invisible. The emperor gave these fellows all the gold they asked for. They, of course, put it away and pretended to be spinning thread, then weaving, cutting, and sewing the material into a splendid suit of clothes for him. Neither the king nor his ministers dared say they couldn't see it. Finally the emperor paraded in his new invisible robes. A child exclaimed, "The king doesn't have any clothes on!" Only then would anybody admit they couldn't see any clothes on him!

Something similar happened with Constantine the Great, emperor of Rome at the beginning of the fourth century. But the consequences were far more serious.

According to the story, in the year A.D. 312 he was fighting off one of his rivals for the imperial throne. Before the battle, Constantine had a vision. A cross appeared in the heavens with the inscription "By this sign, conquer." At the Milvian Bridge several miles out of Rome, under a banner with the same words, his troops were indeed victorious.

After this, Constantine the Great is supposed to have been a Christian. Every year to this day he is celebrated among Greek Christians on May 22 as a great saint.

The emperor had changed his religious clothes, perhaps. Maybe he *did* fool the unwary Christian bishops of his day with his new clothes. Yet down deep inside he was still the same old pagan politician. Spiritually he was still naked. Through all the years after his "conversion" he continued to function as head of Roman pagan religion. He never objected to being worshiped as a god himself. Obviously he wasn't about to quit fighting, no matter what Jesus might have said about enemy-love. His "conversion" did not keep him from murdering a son and wife for political purposes.

So why is he considered a Christian saint? Mainly because he was the first emperor to realize that Christianity was here to stay. He saw that persecuting it was not the way to deal with it. He needed a centralized religion to help unify the state, and thought Christianity would serve this purpose.

By this time, however, Christians were no longer united themselves. Who could settle their differences? Constantine made himself available for umpiring theological squabbles among Christians. Though not baptized as a Christian, the emperor came to regard himself as a bishop for the bishops.

They, of course, were glad enough to have him on their side of an argument instead of against all Christians!

And the Result Is Christendom!

Since pagan Romans regarded the emperor as a god, what would happen when the emperor favored Christianity? Well, eventually the emperors gave up saying they were gods. Yet the church came to believe that their authority to rule came straight from God. While emperors were no longer worshiped as gods, Christians still felt their authority was sacred.

From now on there were two ways for God's will to be known. One was through the church and its teaching. This applied to private morality. The other was through God's appointed "Christian" ruler. And this applied to public policy.

This can happen whenever a general understanding arises that everyone in a society is Christian. Or at least everyone that matters. Certainly the rulers. We call this "Christendom." Christendom permits Christianity to become state policy. The church then no longer needs to allow for the Holy Spirit to convince people how to behave. Rather it can instruct the government to *make* people behave.

As the church takes responsibility for the society at large, suddenly the idea of Christians not taking part in wars seems no longer practical. Such refusal in the Christendom arrangement would totally disarm the nation, it is thought. It would leave it weak and defenseless before enemies who are not Christian. They could take over the government whenever they wanted to do so. Who would stop them?

A new doctrine concerning Christians and war became necessary.

Questions for Reflection and Discussion

1. Since we live "in the world," it is necessary and good that we share many of our ways of thinking with the world. If we didn't, meaningful conversation with the world would be impossible, and the missionary task would grind to a halt. The Bible instructs us to have "the mind of Christ" and warns us against unthinking conformity to the attitudes and thought of the world. How can we tell when concepts we may share with non-Christians are actually incompatible with biblical Christianity?

2. The church remembers its first centuries of existence in the midst of persecution as a golden age of faithfulness under pressure. Yet most Christians also believe that the adoption of Christianity as the official religion of the state was also a great victory. Do you believe it is in the interest of the church to be closely identified with the state? What are some advantages of such an arrangement? What are some disadvantages?

CHAPTER 2

The Legacy of Augustine

For hundreds of years Rome had stood fast, a fortress of civilization. One hundred years after the "conversion" of Constantine, however, the Roman Empire was in deep trouble. The barbarians were invading! Across the borders of the empire everything was rotten. Uncivilized tribes roamed the country. There were no decent laws. People were dirty and lived like animals. Even worse, they were heathen!

By now quite a few Romans were Christian, of course. Even Romans who were still pagan were no longer persecuting Christians. While pagan Romans were immoral, they at least were *nice*.

Eventually the barbarians had invaded as far as the gates of Hippo, a city in Africa on the shore of the Mediterranean Sea. The bishop of the Christian church, a certain Augustine, found himself with a crisis on his hands. Boniface, the general in charge of defending the city, was a Christian.

Now Boniface may well have received the traditional teaching many Christians still held in those days.

The church had generally been teaching that if you became a Christian while in the army you did not have to leave the army. However, you were not allowed to kill anyone.

At any rate, Boniface decided to leave the army and become a monk. Augustine, the Christian bishop, hurried to convince the general to stay on and command the defense of the city against the invaders.

Where could he find arguments to persuade the general? Not in the words of Jesus, of course. Nor in the traditional teaching of the church. So he reached back to Plato and Cicero, the pagan writers. Said Augustine:

> Peace should be the object of your desire; war should be waged only as a necessity, and waged only that God may by it deliver men from the necessity and preserve them in peace. For peace is not sought in order to the kindling of war, but war is waged in order that peace may be obtained. Therefore, even in waging war, cherish the spirit of a peacemaker, that, by conquering those whom you attack, you may lead them back to the advantages of peace.[2]

Augustine was saying that Christians must be very careful to fight only wars that are just. Boniface heard—and it has been understood ever since—that it is all right for Christians to fight. Period.

Augustine Invents the Square Wheel

How do we know what a wheel is? Well, it usually has a place in the middle where it is connected to an axle in order for it to spin around. And it has to be round. It wouldn't always have to be *perfectly* round, but obviously, it couldn't be square. A square wheel would not *work*. It could never function as a wheel, and therefore would not *be* a wheel.

Something similar happens with love. We can identify the presene of love in human relationships because of the way it affects behavior. Take Jesus, for example. Who could doubt the love of Jesus when he acted the way he did?

Augustine had to answer the argument that true Christian love forbids killing the enemy. To do this he turned to something Jesus had once said. Jesus had said that getting angry with someone is the same as murdering him. Augustine understood this to mean that what you *do* is not important. What really matters is how you *feel*.

Christians must always have love in their hearts, of course. Yet there will be times when evil persons break the peace or commit injustice. Since evil persons should not be allowed to get away with their violence, Christians must at times stop them, Augustine thought. Defense against an invading army would be a case in point.

This should not be engaged in with hate, he said. Christians must guard their hearts against "passion." Even while carrying out the demands of justice, they should be moved by love for the enemy. He wrote:

> If to kill a man is murder, this may happen sometimes without any sin. When a soldier kills the enemy, when a judge or an executioner kills the criminal . . . I do not think they sin by killing a man. . . . When a sol-

dier kills the enemy he is enforcing the law, and so
has no difficulty in carrying out his duty without passion.[3]

No one indeed is fit to inflict punishment save the
one who has first overcome hate in his heart. The
love of enemies admits no dispensation, but love does
not exclude wars of mercy waged by the good.[4]

This is a square wheel. It is love that does not do
the kinds of things we recognize as love. If Augustine
is right, people who have overcome hate in their
hearts will end up doing exactly the same things done
by evil people, whose hearts are full of hate. The only
difference is in their hearts, their intentions.

This means there is no such thing as wicked deeds;
only wicked hearts. It makes inner feelings the final
judge of all behavior. It no longer matters *what* you
do, but *why* you do it.

This kind of thinking did not begin with Augustine.
Jesus had already found it among the Pharisees. Some
of them thought they had good reasons for not honor-
ing their parents. They thought they had good reasons
for trying to keep Jesus from healing on the Sabbath,
and even for crucifying him. It is nothing short of
amazing that such reasoning found its way back into
Christian thought.

Other Forms of Acceptable Violence

Augustine faced other problems as well. In his day,
being a bishop in his area was not easy. For a hundred years, the African church had been split into two
rival denominations, the Catholics and the Donatists.

The Catholics agreed with the official religion of the emperor. The Donatists, a local fringe group, had split off from the Catholics over issues of church discipline.

Augustine was in favor of unity. He tried every way he could think of to get the Donatists to become Catholics. He eventually came to believe the only way to unite the church was through force. He had started out thinking it would be wrong for the imperial police to force Donatists to become Catholic. When they did so anyway, Augustine became convinced it had worked for good after all. "Whoever is not found within the church is not to be asked why. He is to be corrected and converted. Or, if brought to book, let him not complain." How were these Christians "brought to book"? It was a shocked pagan who wrote to Augustine concerning the procedure:

> Reflect on the appearance presented by a town from which men doomed to torture are dragged forth; think of the lamentations of mothers and wives, of sons and fathers; think of the shame felt by those who may return, set at liberty indeed, but having undergone the torture.[5]

But it is not only the torture of persons he considered heretics that Augustine found acceptable. In a book he wrote, *The City of God*, Augustine is deeply saddened by the evil world he sees around him. People who are guilty of crime tend to lie about their guilt, he laments. So the only possible way to find out if they are really guilty is to torture them. But, oh sorrow! The person being tortured just might be innocent, after all. Yes, this rotten, sinful world is such that an innocent person must sometimes be tortured. Augustine finds it "unendurable; a thing, indeed to be bewailed, and, if that were possible, watered with fountains of tears." For sometimes, when the torture becomes unbearable, an innocent person will say he is guilty just for the sake of stopping the pain. In the end, then, a person might be both tortured and sentenced to death, and still be innocent.

In the midst of this weeping and wailing, it never seems to cross Augustine's mind that torture itself might be wrong. He never considered that perhaps a Christian should not do it. No, Augustine received much deep comfort from his tears. They showed him that Christian love and compassion were still supreme in his heart.

In a nutshell, then, this is the essence of the thought of Augustine on such matters: A Christian may fight the enemy. A Christian may torture, maim, and kill the enemy. A Christian may even persecute those who disagree with his religion— on three conditions. First, it must be for a just cause. Second, one must truly love one's victims. And third, one must feel great sorrow about the need to behave this way.

Compare all of this to the thought of Paul, the apostle. For him sorrow does not prove love is present. He discovers love where the barriers between Jewish, Greek, barbarian, and Sycthian enemies have disappeared in Christ (Colossians 3:11). With common sense and spiritual insight, he declares quite simply that love does not harm its neighbor. (See Romans 13:10.) How refreshing.

Why Take Augustine Seriously Then?

George Orwell, an English author early in this century, wrote a novel about a make-believe evil government ruling in the year 1984. In his book, the Ministry of Love is where they torture dissidents. The Ministry of Peace is where the generals organize their wars. The Ministry of Truth is where they continually make up new lies to tell the people. The whole system is held together by slogans. These slogans were absolute nonsense, but after hearing them repeated often enough, people came to accept them as profound truths. "War is peace" is one of the more memorable ones.

Augustine would have felt right at home. He could have added a few slogans of his own: "Torture is love." "Religious persecution is Christian brotherhood." "War is justice." "To kill an enemy is to follow Christ."

Why then must we take Augustine seriously? Why devote a whole chapter to his thought? The main reason is that every Christian who says it is okay for Christians to fight depends upon Augustine. Even if they don't always realize it.

Most Christians believe Augustine was a great saint. His writings have influenced many areas of Christian thought. He was brilliant at expressing Christianity in ways people of his time could understand and become excited about. He regularly stood up for traditional Christian values.

But one way or another, Christians were now going to be in government. They were not going to sit back and allow people of inferior beliefs to be in control of society. In this area, Augustine probably did not realize how far he was from the thought of Jesus. He was simply trying to be a responsible Christian under changed circumstances.

Questions for Reflection and Discussion

1. Love is more what a person *does* than how he or she *feels*. Do you understand this statement? Do you agree with it?

2. Much Christian behavior since Augustine has been determined by the principle "the ends justify the means." According to this principle, some actions we wouldn't normally find acceptable are permissible if the expected result is positive enough. Do you think this way of determining right and wrong behavior is correct for Christians? Is there *anything* Christians would stop short of committing if this rule were really followed?

PART TWO

How Most Christians Justify Warfare

CHAPTER 3

Sad But True: Responsible Christians Must Fight

Most Christians since Augustine have felt that certain situations justify their participation in warfare. A number of different arguments have been put forward to explain this position.

In 1976 I met a pastor who had started a church in Argentina. He seemed to be a nice fellow, and I have often wondered what has become of him. I met him at a conference for Christian ministers in that country.

I do not remember how we got on the subject of war. He was a police officer, as well as a Christian minister. He described the attitude with which he proceeded to arrest people.

"Jesus was meek and humble," he explained. "He expressed love when it was appropriate to do so. But he could also express God's justice and judgment when it was necessary. He did not restrain his words in dealing with the Pharisees; and he drove the money changers out of the temple. When I go to make an arrest, I stand straight and let the authority of the Lord of Hosts shine in my face. I put the fear of God in criminals. They must know they have not only violated the laws of man, but also stand under the wrath of God."

It has since come to light that in those years, tens of thousands of normal Argentine citizens "disappeared" from their homes. They were brutally tortured, raped, even thrown live out of airplanes into the sea. The tragedy of those years has been well documented. I will not dwell on it here. Sometimes I wonder if this brother still feels it was appropriate in those years to execute the wrath—as well as the mercy and love—of God.

Probably so. Christians normally believe that the love and the justice of God go hand in hand. Because God is love, God does not stop being just. Many Christians would then add that love is an insufficient force in dealing with real evil in the real world. It is proper for Christians to forgive certain kinds of personal offenses. But some kinds of evil no individual Christian has a right to forgive, they argue. Too many others are affected by it.

Yes, love and forgiveness can resolve many kinds of conflict. But what is love and forgiveness against a Hitler? God's demand for justice and righteousness must be taken seriously. God has established punishment for the unrepentant evildoer. And ever since early Old Testament times, God's punishment has occasionally taken the form of war.

It is said that Christians must not be afraid to distinguish between good and evil. They must stand up courageously for righteousness. God has established government to punish the evildoer. God established the death penalty. God does not hesitate to use force to stop evil. God has often used wars to punish evil nations. We dare not believe that trust in the deliverance of the Lord means passive inaction in the face of evil. Where does the Bible say we must sit idle while evil goes unpunished?

Some Christians even say that the nuclear destruction of the world might at some point be a proper expression of this justice and wrath of the Lord. It is to be preferred to the victory of a godless and injust aggressor over a spinelessly passive Christian nation, they argue.

Sometimes It Is Impossible to Avoid Evil

Another viewpoint is accepted by many Christians. They admit that often the steps taken to punish evildoers have evil consequences as well. So what are we supposed to do? Wring our hands and do nothing? Doing nothing, however, may actually be the greater evil! It often is.

We may even face a decision in which everything we might do—or not do—will have some evil consequences, they declare. At such times, we must carefully consider which action will produce less evil. Sometimes fighting a war will be just such a lesser evil. Granted, evil and injustice will be committed in the course of the war. But anything else we might do would be much worse.

Pacifism Is Irrelevant

Irrelevant is a word we use for something which is not related to the situation at hand. Of course, people often do not agree on what is irrelevant in a certain discussion.

For example, let's consider the position some Christians take against defending their country. They base their action on the belief that to love as Jesus loved means we cannot bear arms against national enemies.

Most Christians dismiss this as an irrelevant position in any serious discussion of national affairs. They believe these ideas are so clearly useless there is no need to consider them. Such ideas can be held only by people who live in some fantasy world where such things are possible. Therefore, those of us who live in the real world can safely ignore such advice.

But wait a minute! Does God want the advice of Christians to be ignored? Of course not! Christians must avoid making silly statements, and shoulder the responsibility of giving sound advice in the real world. It is more important to offer relevant support for a responsible national policy than to be slavishly faithful to the thought of Jesus, these Christians believe.

Government and the Individual Have Different Duties

Not all Christians who believe it is sometimes proper for Christians to fight think of it as a lesser evil. They prefer to think of it as a lesser good. It is an unpleasant, but still necessary, good action. There is nothing in it to worry the Christian conscience.

It is somewhat like spanking a child. As with correcting a child, however, it is not proper for just anyone to spank him. It must be that child's proper authority—a parent or perhaps a schoolteacher. What might be wrong for just anybody, then, is proper if the right person does it.

A fundamental principle for most Christians since Augustine concerns the difference between the individual and government. They believe the Bible says clearly that God created national governments to carry out justice. A government which does not punish evil is in fact rebelling against God. If a government refused to defend its citizens, it would only invite disorder. God created government in the first place to avoid disorder.

Now what God created cannot be wrong! For a duly constituted authority to defend the citizens of the nation cannot be a sin, these Christians say. The ruler is only carrying out God's intention in creating government. How could carrying out God's intention be a sin? And if it is not a sin, if there is nothing wrong with it, there is nothing to keep a Christian from it, they conclude.

These Christians believe there are things a Christian must never do on his or her own. As a private person, one may never destroy one's enemy, refuse loving forgiveness, refuse to turn the other cheek. But if one happens to be the authority established to punish evil, things are different. In doing this, one is carrying out God's will for one's office.

The Importance of the State in Protestant Thought

Martin Luther believed that what a Christian individual may *not* do, the state *must*. And he went one step further. Within this God-created order of things, the duty of the normal citizen is obedience. The Bible says that to resist the government is to resist God. If the government says to fight in a war, a Christian dare not disobey. Unless, of course, one knows clearly that the war in question is unjust. Still, the Christian had best give government the benefit of the doubt. It is better to err on the side of obedience than of rebellion.

Luther also believed that a mercenary performs a proper Christian function. As someone who fights for pay and adventure, this person is no different from a carpenter or a farmer. Both are earning a living. Yes, it involves torturing and maiming people, killing and destroying human life. But so long as it is done in the service of some properly constituted authority, it is fitting for Christians, Luther taught.

Luther had no reason to doubt government authority. He lived more than a thousand years after Augustine. The marriage between church and state begun by Constantine the Great was even older.

One thing mattered to Luther above all else: To purify the church of God from everything that made people think they had to earn salvation. He had discovered that God loves to forgive sin. As Luther gave himself to making this known again, he found willing help in certain rulers. Like the emperor in the days of Augustine, the princes of the small German states helped him to fight for true religion. His Reformation depended on the backing and protection of the state.

Luther was deeply grateful. Did these German noblemen need to fight wars? Luther was not about to

stand in their way. At one point, the German peas-
antry rose up against their oppressors, the very
princes who supported the Reformation. Luther came
down clearly on the side of the authorities. He
strongly encouraged them to put down the rebellion
with any means necessary.

> It is pitiful that we have to be so cruel to the poor
> people, but what can we do? It is necessary and God
> wills it that fear may be brought on the people.
> Otherwise, Satan brings forth mischief. . . . Hence-
> forth, the peasants will know how wrong they were
> and perhaps leave off rioting, or at least do it less. Do
> not be troubled about their suffering, for it will profit
> many souls.[6]

In practice, Luther's reverence for "authority"
grants the rich and powerful a God-given right to use
whatever force is necessary to remain in power.

John Calvin, another important Reformation figure,
also lived in terror of what would happen if law and
order broke down. This was not a personal fear. Calvin was probably not afraid of martyrdom. However,
he could not bear to think of disorder or the break-
down of civil society. If good, righteous, Christian
people refused to exercise force to guarantee an
orderly society, nothing but evil would result.

In this area, Catholic and Protestant thought agrees.
Augustine's thought lies behind what Catholics think
about warfare to this day. The Protestant Reform-
ers—Luther, Calvin, and the rest—were also convinced Augustine was right.

Laying Down Rules for Justified War

Obviously, no serious Christian would say that fighting is *always* okay. Ever since Augustine, concerned Christians have tried to spell out exactly what situations justify warfare. Some have given a lot of thought to laying down certain rules to help a Christian decide. Though they have never made an officially adopted statement that may be followed, their arguments follow similar lines. We may sum them up in four simple points.

1. Only a properly constituted authority may fight a war. This is not a matter for private individuals to take into their own hands. The individual Christian, in personal life, must love the enemy as Jesus commanded.

2. Wars may be fought only for a just cause. Exactly what makes a cause just is not always clear. In practice, the theory that certain wars are justified relies on common sense. Both British and Argentine Christians believed they had just cause for fighting over the Falkland/Malvinas Islands in 1982. Most German Christians considered Nazi expansionism a just cause for World War II. Yet Christians in other nations considered it a just cause to stop them.

3. Wars must be fought in proper ways. Certain kinds of weapons and certain ways of treating prisoners or civilians are too inhumane to be allowed. An important concern in this regard is that of "proportionality." The evil committed must never be greater than the evil it means to avoid or punish.

Some Christians, concerned about the possibility of a nuclear holocaust, are afraid others may believe war is now so unthinkable that it is no longer a real possibility. Still, a "third generation" of nuclear arms is now supposed to be able to destroy only selected military targets. The secondary, uncontrolled destruction we usually associate with nuclear weapons will be controlled. If the new technology works as stated, it should make nuclear weapons acceptable to Christians who have objected to them up to now, they say.

4. The attitudes in fighting must be correct. Selfishness, greed, pride, hatred, revenge, the delight in hurting others—these are not proper motives for Christians to do *anything*. Certainly to fight wars in such a spirit is wrong.

In the next few chapters we will look at the various ways in which this line of thought, often called "the just-war theory," has developed.

Questions for Reflection and Discussion

1. Do you agree that a consistently pacifist, defenseless opinion is irrelevant in any responsible discussion of national policy? Is relevance an important factor in deciding whether an opinion is correct? Is it possible for Christians to hold *any* belief to be correct, if it must be measured by the world's standards of relevance?

2. An important distinction in the thought of many Christians is that a Christian public official *must*, as a public official, do some things a Christian *may not* do as a private person. Is this always true? Is it ever true? Why or why not? If it is true, would you be willing to serve in public office, or would you disqualify yourself?

CHAPTER 4

Against the Violence of the Oppressor

Let us suppose you were born in South Africa with black skin. Most of the people around you are like you—black-skinned. The few white-skinned people in the country own the best land. They own the factories, the gold and diamond mines, the schools. They own the future of your country. They own your future. Your wife and family must live in one of the "homelands" far from where you grew up. You work the mines and may come home to visit once or twice a year.

Again let us suppose you were born poor in Latin America. You may live halfway up one of the hills that surround a huge city. It's a smelly half-hour walk up from the nearest water source, from the nearest "street," past rows and rows of shanties put together with scraps of wood, tar paper, and flattened-out five-liter tin cans.

Suppose you are a child whose mother abandoned you one day in a large city, rather than watch you starve. In some third-world cities, gangs of such children grow up on what they can beg or steal. Nearby, the rich live in joyful indifference. High-rise buildings go up. Glittering cars speed around you. Down by the beach, luxury hotels cater to rich tourists. Factories belch black smoke. Here your country's resources are processed for export.

Perhaps you are a peasant asking for land, needing land. Just a patch of land to produce enough to eat. But the few families who own the land control the army and the government. Perhaps you have been arrested and tortured because one day you were in a crowd shouting slogans and pleading for land. Your brother-in-law has "disappeared." Maybe tonight they'll come for you.

Injustice. You know it well if you live in one of the above situations. Or you may meet it in other, more subtle ways in the place where you live.

When Is War Against Authority Not Sin?

"God is just. God's love does not stop God from punishing the wicked. Christians must not stand idly in the face of injustice and wickedness. They must stand up for righteousness." Many Christians have given this as a reason for going to war.

Yet traditional Christian thought states that a war can be just only when fought by a properly con-stituted authority. Private citizens must not take revenge into their own hands. When German peasants revolted against the harsh "nobility" in the sixteenth century, Luther was shocked. He felt a principle of divine order had been violated.

Somehow this contradiction must be resolved. Is

revolutionary war *never* right? Against the evil and injustice of Hitler, Christians of the world mobilized their armies and resources. It took years of terrible war to stop Hitler, but they felt justified for having destroyed the wicked Nazi system. Yet, while in Europe and North America the grain bins overflow and the stockpiles of butter turn rancid, people elsewhere die of starvation. As the months come and go, the number of those who starve adds up to more than all the Jews Hitler ever killed.

Will Christians do battle against the new Hitlers of economic oppression? Will they avenge this daily destruction as well? Does not the wrath and justice of God call for total annihilation of this wicked system of twisted priorities? This sick system by which the rich continue to strip away the land, the natural resources, the rights, the very life of the poor?

Thomas Aquinas was a famous Christian theologian in the late Middle Ages. At one point in his writings he addressed the issue of whether it is sin to fight against an oppressive government. He had already established that, as a rule, revolution ("sedition," he calls it) is a mortal sin. Yet faced with such a government he argues as follows:

> A tyrannical government is not just, because it is directed, not to the common good, but to the private good of the ruler. . . . Consequently, there is no sedition in disturbing a government of this kind. . . . Indeed, it is the tyrant rather that is guilty of sedition, since he encourages discord and sedition among his subjects, that he may lord over them more securely;

for this is tyranny, being conducive to the private good of the ruler, and to the injury of the multitude.[7]

John Locke, who wrote toward the end of the seventeenth century, spelled out a similar argument. That century had seen England revolt against the king and live without a monarch for almost two decades. Christians were very much involved in that experiment. The whole upheaval had been over religion. So when John Locke wrote 30 years later, he was only elaborating upon things Christians in England had been thinking about for years.

Suppose someone comes to power by means other than those which have been legally established. Under such circumstances, the new ruler, Locke argued, has no real claim to power until the people of the country have given their consent. To revolt against such a ruler in defense of the rightfully appointed one is not wrong, he said. Furthermore,

> Whosoever uses force without right—as everyone does in society who does it without law—puts himself into a state of war with those against whom he so uses it, and in that state all former ties are canceled, all other rights cease, and everyone has a right to defend himself, and to resist the aggressor.[8]

Thus, according to Locke, it is the oppressive, unjust governments who have started the war. Christians who believe fighting is justified only when declared by a proper authority, state another principle: Wars of unprovoked aggression are always wrong. Defense against such aggression is always justified, they say. Therefore when people defend themselves by fighting against oppression, they are waging a just war.

Latin America Today: A Case in Point

Camilo Torres, a Catholic priest in Colombia, in our own century, is considered by many a true martyr for the Christian faith. He identified with the poor. He saw their suffering, their misery. He realized that "charity," the usual Christian approach to poverty, provided no solutions. Nothing really changes when the poor receive a few items of hand-me-down clothing or cans of powdered milk. The whole economic and political system is designed to keep the rich in power and the poor in misery. Camilo Torres came to believe that saying mass was an insufficient expression of his love for his people. He joined the war for their liberation and was killed.

For him, as for Locke, it is the will of the people which determines the legitimacy of government:

> The minority is not handing over the government, and that is undemocratic. If we are the majority, if we really are a democracy and really believe in democracy, we are the ones who must rule. If the minority injures democracy, through violence, let them know we will answer violence with violence.[9]

Many other concerned Christians in Latin America today agree with Torres and with Locke. The oppressive authorities have used violence first. Violence is being committed continually by the system. To refuse to take sides in favor of the war for liberation in Latin

America because of a supposed distaste for violence is sheer hypocrisy, they say. Violence is already there—the violence of oppression. It results in real death. If you are unwilling to resist it you are supporting it, they say. There can be no neutrality in the current struggle for liberation.

According to these persons, class conflict exists because the rich and powerful have taken the initiative in exploiting the poor. Class conflict does not exist because Karl Marx and the communists say it does; they merely describe reality. It is the violence of the rich which causes class conflict.

Gustavo Gutierrez is a concerned Christian theologian in Latin America. Like Augustine hundreds of years before, he also wishes to ensure no loss of Christian love in the conflict:

> The gospel announces the love of God toward all and asks us to love as God loves, but to accept class conflict means to choose to be in favor of some and against others. To live both things without getting them confused is a great challenge for the Christian who is committed to the totality of the liberation process. . . . Universal love is that which in solidarity with the oppressed seeks also to liberate the oppressors from their own power, their ambition, and their selfishness. . . . The oppressors are loved in liberating them from their own inhuman situation as such, liberating them from themselves. But no one can arrive at this except by resolutely taking sides with the oppressed, that is, by fighting against the oppressor class. To really and efficaciously fight, not to hate; this is the challenge, as new as the gospel: to love the enemy.[10]

Very profound. One expresses love by stripping the enemy of the possibility of commiting further injustice. In the process, of course, the enemy will be destroyed. When we saw this line of reasoning in Augustine, we called it a square wheel. People are still trying to ride it.

In right-wing Christian thought, *might makes right*. Those in authority are who God wants in authority because God is in control of history. The fact that they are in power shows they should be in power.

In left-wing Christian thought, *right makes might*. Christians engage in armed struggle for a better system in the faith that, since they are working for justice, God will eventually grant them the victory.

In the New Testament, *might is merely might*. The mighty—right or wrong—will perish by the sword they have lived by. The meek will inherit the earth. This is certainly no blank check for those in power to do as they please. On the other hand, it does not grant the oppressed a God-given right to rise up in arms. God will use *other* means to accomplish God's purposes.

Questions for Reflection and Discussion

1. "It is impossible to remain neutral in the presence of injustice. If you do not engage in positive action for the sake of the oppressed, you are participating in the violence of the oppressor." Do you agree with this statement? If this *is* true, what does it say about you?

2. How far may a Christian go in defending those who suffer innocently? Is it legitimate to set limits to this kind of activity? Does God set such limits?

CHAPTER 5

When God Commands It

In 1095, Pope Urban II launched the first crusade to seize Palestine—"the Holy Land"—from the Turks. His words were full of religious authority as he expressed a new theology of warfare for Christians:

> Most beloved brethren, moved by the exigencies of the times, I, Urban, wearing by permission of God the papal tiara, and spiritual ruler of the whole world, have come to you, the servants of God, as a messenger to disclose the divine admonition. . . . You must carry succor to your brethren dwelling in the East. . . . For the Turks, a Persian people, have attacked them. . . . Wherefore, I pray and exhort, nay not I, but the Lord prays and exhorts you, as heralds of Christ, by frequent exhortation, to urge men of all ranks, knights and foot soldiers, rich and poor, to hasten to exterminate this vile race from the lands of our brethren, and to bear timely aid to the worshippers of Christ. I speak to those who are present, I proclaim to the absent, but Christ commands. Moreover, the sins of those who set out thither, if they lose their lives on the journey, by land or sea, or in fight-

ing against the heathen, shall be remitted in that hour; this I grant to all who go, through the power of God vested in me.[11]

We have come a long way from Augustine. We have come a long way from caring Christians who seek an end to injustice in an oppressed world. Gone is the reluctance, the sadness in the face of the violence to be committed. Gone is the attempt to love the enemy, if only inwardly. This is a war of extermination. This "Persian people" is a "vile race," which must be wiped from the face of the earth on religious, cultural, and ultimately racial grounds.

Why? How could Christians have come to such a ghastly attitude? Because, if we are to believe Pope Urban II, "Christ commands it." Evidently most Christians of the time thought this was true. They actually believed Christ himself was commanding Christians to fight the Turks. And if it was Christ who was commanding, it became a simple matter of obedience. All other considerations had to be abandoned.

When Old Testament War Becomes the Model

We mentioned in the first chapter that most Christian understandings of war come from paganism. We have noticed the influence of thinkers like Plato and Cicero upon Augustine. He in turn influenced many others.

We must observe now, however, the influence of Old Testament holy war upon some Christians. This goes in the opposite direction from pagan influence. Pagan philosophers had argued for moderation. They sought peace and justice and held to a code of honor in warfare. But the model of Old Testament holy war has inspired in some Christians a spirit of fanaticism and intolerance. This spirit has opened the way to untempered destruction.

What lay behind Israel's problems with the Canaanite population? The Bible says Israel's own unfaithfulness caused most of the problems. But one of the marks of this unfaithfulness was the failure to utterly destroy the Canaanite population in the first place. God had commanded complete destruction of the Palestinian population. King Saul lost God's approval because he spared some of God's enemies from the slaughter.

Some of us would question whether this is the proper way to interpret these Old Testament passages. But that is not our subject right now. The fact is that the Scriptures are normally understood this way. And the result has at times been inspiration for killing a whole race of people.

Some New England Puritan preachers in the seventeenth and eighteenth centuries called native Americans "Amalekites." They, the Puritans, were a new Israel, of course. God had led them to the promised land of America. Now he expected them to deal with the native population much as he had commanded Israel to deal with the Amalekites in Canaan. Unlike the experience of the Old Testament, the genocide in North America was largely "successful."

The Influence of Islam

For many centuries Christians did not believe the warfare commanded in the Old Testament had any direct relation to their own wars. Two obstacles stood in the way. First, the teaching of Jesus continued to have a tempering influence, even when Christians were able to justify fighting under certain circumstances. Second, a clear commandment of God to eliminate the enemy had to be established. For over a thousand years after Christ, no one dared to claim a clear commandment from God to fight as Joshua or Saul had received.

How did Christians come to believe God was again actually *commanding* them to fight? Jacques Ellul of France is an influential Christian writer. In a recent book he stated his belief that the decisive influence in this direction came from Islam. The strong belief of Islam in holy war has again been demonstrated for the world in recent Iranian history. The news media have reported the fanatical cult of war shown by the Iranians: the Islamic *jihad*. It was highly visible in their revolution against the Shah and especially in their war against Iraq.

Why were thousands and thousands of Iranians so willing—eager, it seems—to lose their lives in war? In the Muslim theology of *jihad*, or holy war, to die in battle is a sacred martyrdom which earns immediate entry into Paradise. Ellul writes,

> The idea of a holy war is a direct product of the Muslim *jihad*. If the latter is a holy war, then obviously the fight against Muslims to defend or save Chris-

tianity has *also* to be a holy war. . . . The Crusade is
an imitation of the *jihad*. Thus the Crusade includes a
guarantee of salvation. The one who dies in a holy
war goes straight to Paradise, and the same applies to
the one who takes part in a Crusade. This is no coin-
cidence; it is an exact equivalent.[12]

For a thousand years, Christians had had the use of
the Old Testament. Yet it never occurred to them to
apply to their own situation God's commandments to
fight in the Old Testament. Once again, the influence
of non-Christian thought had shaped a Christian
understanding of war.

The Crusading Spirit in the Americas

We have mentioned that some early North
American Christians thought their war to exterminate
the native population was a holy cause. This mentality
has continued to exert its influence upon many Christians in the United States. For many Northerners, the
abolition of slavery was a holy cause. The "Battle
Hymn of the Republic," a popular song of the Civil
War, says,

> I have read a fiery gospel writ in burnished rows of
>   steel:
> "As ye deal with My contemners, so with you My
>   grace shall deal":
> Let the Hero born of woman crush the serpent with
>   His heel,
> Since God is marching on.
>
> He has sounded forth the trumpet that shall never
>   call retreat;

> He is sifting out the hearts of men before His judg-
> ment seat.
> Oh, be swift, my soul, to answer Him! Be jubilant, my
> feet!
> Our God is marching on.[13]

When the United States joined the fighting in World War I, the same crusading spirit was heard from many pulpits across the nation. And then 20 years later, God obviously was interested in Hitler's destruction, right? And, of course, is not the destruction of "Godless communism" also a sacred duty, a holy cause? "Kill a commie for Christ" was a slogan during the war in Vietnam.

At the opposite end of the political spectrum, the crusading spirit is evident among some Christians in Latin America. They believe God commands the Marxist-inspired revolution there.

Ernesto Cardenal, a priest, became Minister of Culture for the Sandinista government of Nicaragua after the defeat of Somoza, the right-wing dictator. Cardenal has written the following dialogue about Jesus chasing the money changers out of the temple:

> Felipe: He taught above all with his example, chasing out the businessmen and bankers, teaching us that it is necessary to be done with the exploitation of man by man. Even if it takes a whip.
>
> Someone asks, grinning: With a whip, but not with an automatic rifle?

Felipe: Even if it takes a whip or an automatic rifle.

Alejo: Whatever it takes. Because the exploitation that Capitalism makes of our bodies is a greater desecration than that of the temple.

Myself: In another commentary of the gospel, I recently read an interesting bit of information. No one was allowed into the temple with weapons or sticks. Therefore, the only weapon Jesus could use there was the one he did use. The Gospel of John says he took cords, and made a whip with them. It is more logical to think many whips were made.

Esperanza: And the fact that Jesus healed the sick there reminds me of Che [an Argentine guerrilla fighter who fought with Castro in Cuba and was finally killed by government troops in Bolivia]. A guerrilla himself, he would stop in the midst of a battle to heal the people because he was a medical doctor.

Olivia: Che and others like Che are like Christ. They are very much like Christ. They are the ones who are purifying the temple of businessmen and exploiters.[14]

Thus is Jesus turned into a Latin-American guerrilla fighter. When the Gospels are read this way, Christ commands—by his example if not with his words—the war for liberation from oppressive capitalism. This war, too, becomes a sacred duty.

Meanwhile, conservative forces in the churches, both Catholic and Protestant, enjoin the authorities to defend themselves against the guerrillas. They follow the tradition of Augustine and Luther, of course. Curiously, Christians of a military mind-set, whether rightist or leftist in their political views, do agree on one thing. It is God's express will that they kill each other!

Questions for Reflection and Discussion

1. Think of the way God has dealt with you in your sins and moral failures. Do you expect the God you have experienced in your personal life will ever command the people of another nation to kill the people of your nation (including you and your family) because of your nation's sins? Does this apply to other nations as well?

2. Think of the Christian doctrine of salvation by grace through the blood of Jesus, as you have understood it. Do you believe Christians might ever earn salvation by participating in a war God might command?

CHAPTER 6

But What About Nuclear War?

At this point in our survey of Christian thought on warfare, it is possible to have developed a mistaken impression. You may be thinking that all Christians are willing to resort rapidly to force and violence as a solution to international or civil conflict. This is not true.

At the end of Chapter 3, we mentioned the just-war theory. These general rules have developed over the years. Their purpose is to try to set limits on Christian participation in war. A justifiable war requires:

1. Properly constituted authority.

2. Just cause.

3. Justice in the way Christians go about their fighting.

4. Proper attitudes.

The preceding chapter, examining the possibility that God might order us to fight, indirectly treated most of these points. If God commands the war, proper authority is established. Under such circumstances, the justice of the cause is self-evident. Proper attitudes? Why, obedience to the command of the Lord is surely sufficient, isn't it?

Chapter 4 dealt with the issue of proper authority and tested the borders of just cause (points 1 and 2 above). But we must still deal with the matter of *means*, point 3.

How may Christians rightly fight? Perhaps as some Christians claim, the punishment carried out through war is morally equivalent to spanking a child. Yet, no parents would bomb, machine-gun, and napalm their entire neighborhood just to make sure their child was punished for a misdeed. No matter what the child had done.

Punishment—at home and in war—must be proportional to the action being punished. It must not cause more harm or injustice than that which is being prevented or punished. It must not harm the innocent. It must not destroy the ecological balance beyond its capacity to heal itself. Its chief aim is to attain an acceptable peace, a better peace than that which existed before. Its purpose is not the annihilation of the other, but the establishment of a peaceful relationship with the adversary.

It is easy to understand, therefore, why some Christians believe nuclear warfare presents special moral problems. Christian reservations concerning nuclear weapons—as well as chemical and biological weapons—fit into another old tradition: being critical of certain wars or weapons without totally rejecting warfare.

The Tradition Against Excessive Violence

Even when Christianity had largely forsaken its original principles for opposing war, certain symbolic signs remained. It did not seem right for clerics to fight. For many years, anyone who had shed blood was refused admittance into monastic orders. Christians who shed blood, even in a justified war, were often required to do penance. Communion was often withheld from them for some time.

In spite of what "noblemen" and authorities were doing, most people were usually spared from actual fighting. Since there was no universal draft as we now know it, most people were free to practice the original Christian teaching against violence. Most Christians were not allowed to return evil for evil.

Even those who could not escape military involvement were encouraged to put a limit on their violence. Note the following oath, sworn by Robert the Pious, king of France between the years 996 and 1031:

> I will not infringe on the Church in any way. I will not hurt a cleric or a monk if unarmed. I will not steal an ox, cow, pig, sheep, goat, ass, or a mare with colt. I will not attack a vilain [farm-worker] or vilainesse or servants or merchants for ransom. I will not take a mule or a horse male or female or a colt in pasture from any man from the calends of March to the feast of All Saints unless to recover a debt. I will not burn houses or destroy them unless there is a knight inside. I will not root up vines. I will not attack noble ladies traveling without husband nor their maids, nor widows or nuns unless it is their fault. From the

> beginning of Lent to the end of Easter I will not attack an unarmed knight.[15]

Perhaps this "limitation" on the excess of war strikes you as not very radical. Yet, some Christian preacher had the courage to bring the principle of self-restraint in warfare to the very king of France!

Erasmus was one of the most influential thinkers of the early sixteenth century. When he addressed the matter of warfare, he wondered why Christians must forever be quoting Augustine rather than Jesus. He could agree that in theory there might be justifiable wars. Yet in practice, he found it difficult to imagine one. He also recognized that situations often arise in which it is not easy to determine who is really in the right. Usually both sides in a war can legitimately claim to be defending justice.

So Erasmus began to suspect there must be some flaw in the way princes go about deciding when to fight.

> The Christian prince should first question his own right, and then if it is established without a doubt he should carefully consider whether it should be maintained by means of catastrophes to the whole world. . . . But what is safe anywhere while everyone is maintaining his rights to the last ditch? We see wars arise from wars, wars following wars, and no end or limit to the upheaval! It is certainly obvious that nothing is accomplished by these means. Therefore, other remedies should be given a trial.[16]

If Justice Is Truly the Objective

In recent generations, Christians have often pushed for international regulations concerning the conduct of war. The very language used by Christians to justify wars calls for international organizations to stop wars. What language? The language of the courtroom.

If wars are justified on the grounds of redressing injustice, of punishing unpardonable evil, then the method must be just and fair as well. It would never do, in normal law, for the same individual to be plaintiff, judge, and executioner. No, the suit must be pressed before a truly impartial judge. This does not happen in war, of course. The aggrieved party takes justice into his or her own hands. This we would never permit in private life.

If the World Court were really respected as such, there would never again be a war. At the most, we would have some kind of United Nations force doing international police duty.

These arguments are not exclusively Christian. But they do stem directly from a certain way in which Christians since Augustine have regarded warfare.

The Case for Nuclear Pacifism

But we inevitably turn again to the issue of nuclear weapons. Are they just another weapon, like the switch from arrows and swords to gunpowder? Or do they represent a totally new moral problem?

Arthur F. Holmes, a Christian writer, has dedicated much thought to the issue. He is no pacifist. He believes strongly that wars are justified for Christians under certain circumstances. His answer to the problem posed by nuclear weapons is quite different, however.

> The horrendously disastrous nature of a nuclear holocaust, spreading death and destruction across large segments of the globe, far exceeds any proportionality to just ends. Yet nuclear attacks on cities would destroy not only military capability, but also medical capability, the economy and the political system, in addition (directly or indirectly) to the majority of a nation's population. All this far exceeds any moral ends for going to war and makes sheer mockery of any notion of justice or love.[17]

He then goes on to propose nuclear disarmament. Even if it must be unilateral (that is, only one side getting rid of the weapons). Even if it means the possiblity of defeat.

> No matter how one regards Communism, it would be morally preferable in the final analysis for us all to be red than for hundreds and hundreds of millions to be dead, while survivors struggle for existence in a fallout-saturated world devoid of any effective economic or political order or medical resources.[18]

A growing number of Christians are expressing similar sentiments. And not only about nuclear weapons. Ever since World War I, people have been horrified by chemical weapons. And again, something similar might be said about the uses of bacteria in warfare.

Something in the heart of concerned Christians refuses to agree to the destruction for which their governments are planning. How tragic if Christian politicians and taxpayers in the United States achieve through nuclear war what the communists have so far failed to do: the total extermination of the 40 million practicing Christians in the Soviet Union. Such a war would also kill—directly or indirectly—just about every other Christian on the face of this earth.

It is true that some of the older weapons with outdated technology are now being destroyed. The destruction of these arms affords occasion for political grandstanding. In reality, however, the arms race will continue furiously. Nobody will stop researching and developing the technology for newer and "better" weapons, nuclear and nonnuclear. Because of Hiroshima and Nagasaki we can imagine the horror of nuclear war. But we can't *imagine* what war with the next generation of weapons will be like.

Questions for Reflection and Discussion

1. Some Christians claim that the nuclear deterrent has effectively enforced peace for several decades. But other Christians contend that the world has not experienced total nuclear destruction only because of God's own care for humanity. Do you believe the world is better off because of the existence of nuclear weapons?

2. Some have suggested that "nuclear pacifism" may be a factor in the development of newer and scarier technology for warfare—that is, that the Strategic Defense Initiative (star wars) received some of its impetus from nuclear pacifists. Do you agree?

CHAPTER 7

When We Don't Stop to Think Carefully

In Mark Twain's humorous novel, *The Adventures of Huckleberry Finn*, Huck and Jim have an accident with their raft on the Mississippi River. After Huck is taken in by the Grangerford family, he finds out about the feud between the Grangerfords and the Shepherdsons.

"What's a feud?"

"Why, where was you raised? Don't you know what a feud is?"

"Never heard of it before—tell me about it."

"Well," says Buck, "a feud is this way: A man has a quarrel with another man, and kills him; then that other man's brother kills *him*; then the other brothers, on both sides, goes for one another; then the *cousins* chip in—and by and by everybody's killed off, and

there ain't no more feud. But it's kind of slow, and
takes a long time."[19]

The following Sunday they go to church. It turns
out the Grangerfords and Shepherdsons go to the
same church. They all take their guns along, and hold
them between their knees or lean them against the
wall where they will be handy if needed.

And then comes what appears to be a note of hope.
The minister preaches a sermon on brotherly love,
and we can see a way to prevent the bitter ending
Buck has foreseen.

The Grangerfords are impressed with the sermon.
They talk it over approvingly on their way home from
church. Presumably, it has had the same effect on the
Shepherdsons. But then that night, the Grangerfords
and Shepherdsons go at each other again, and no one
survives the slaughter.

As one reads the careful writing of Christians on
the matter of war, one can gain the impression that
they represent how most Christians actually think and
act. Nothing could be further from the truth. The true
attitudes of most Christians in times of war are as
unreflective and emotional as those of the Grangerfords and Shepherdsons.

Most Christians in the face of war have not thought
through their attitudes carefully. Christian teaching
has had a minimal effect in determining how they will
actually behave when war breaks out. Too often
people who claim to follow the Bible are selfish,
violent, and judgmental. The high ideals of Christian
teaching often make no difference in real behavior.

When Preachers Have Not Thought About It

If we observe carefully, we will notice that the attitudes of the preachers themselves are often unreflective. They have seldom given careful consideration to the issues at stake. They have often assumed—because their own teachers had always assumed—that the teaching of Jesus is of secondary importance in this matter. That in this area—in just this one area—it is necessary to obey *other persons* rather than God.

All they know is that, for as long as anyone can remember, Christians have always taken part in war. Every major Christian denomination believes some wars are justified. And if this is the way the preachers think, why should anyone bother to raise questions?

As a matter of fact, many new Christians do raise questions. New Christians often display a special sensitivity to the Holy Spirit. The book of Revelation calls this "first love" (2:4). For this reason, people in the military often have questions about their profession after they become followers of Christ. And at that point, Christian ministers reassure them that their scruples are unnecessary.

Are these ministers resisting the Spirit? Perhaps, but not intentionally. It is just that they themselves have never been taught to expect the teaching of Jesus to be relevant at this point.

A Secondary Issue

The line of thinking many Christians follow goes something like this: Some doctrines are important, others less so. How then do we know which ones are important? Only small, marginal denominations teach

Christian opposition to all wars as a principle. There-fore, such Christian pacifism must be a small, marginal doctrine.

They reason that if pacifism were really a neces-sary, primary doctrine, the Holy Spirit would have revealed it to the many sincere Christians who seek the Lord in all their doings. If pacifism is essential, they say, how can one explain God's blessing on non-pacifist Christian groups? How can one explain their growth, their experience of miracles? How can one explain the successful ministry of so many church leaders upon whom the power of God clearly rests? Think of all the Christian saints and martyrs through the ages who were not pacifists! Are Mennonites, Quakers, and other pacifists ready to dismiss the wit-ness and ministry of nonpacifists because of this one issue?

Many pacifist Christians would not go that far. But then, doesn't that show this really is a secondary mat-ter? Why raise the unnecessary stumbling block of pacifism? Faithfulness to this peculiar, marginal doc-trine gets in the way of what is really important, they believe. Here's what is really important: The mission-ary commission for expansive, Spirit-filled, effective evangelism in unity with all other devout Christians.

In this manner, Christians avoid examining the issue itself. They decide there is no need to examine the Scriptures on the subject. In fact they won't even bother with Augustine or with just-war theory. Even *that* might put limits on their approval of war.

How Do Most Christians Really Decide Which Wars Are Justified?

As a matter of fact, most Christians don't decide. They just "know." I mean, if the Soviets start sending their missiles over, what are we supposed to do? Sit down and study what a bunch of theologians have said about war?

Or if the rich landholders fence off our land. Or if the British refuse even to talk about sovereignty of the Malvinas Islands. Or if. . . .

Christians "decide" a war is just when the news media that inform them decide a war is just. They decide it is proper to fight when the government says it is proper. "I mean, surely *they* know why it is necessary to fight! *They* have all the information. *They* have been trying to settle things peacefully, sometimes for years. We can't have every citizen trying to second-guess the government, trying to run their own independent foreign policy, can we? Who are *we* to decide the question? Leave it to the experts. That's what we have government for, anyway. It is their duty to run the country, and it is the Christian's duty to submit and obey."

Not everyone would say it as crassly. Yet the attitude is often that of the United States patriot who exclaimed, "May she always be in the right; but our country, right or wrong!"

That phrase aptly symbolizes a surrender of Christian responsibility. Unfortunately, people are usually unwilling to discern the difference between good and evil once war has been declared. This unwillingness reflects a lack of allegiance to the Lord of lords and King of kings.

Questions for Reflection and Discussion

1. How many Christians do you know, outside of traditional "peace churches," who have carefully thought about this issue? Is this a true indicator of the importance of the subject in the eyes of God? If biblical pacifism is more important to God than this would indicate, how do you explain the silence of most great church leaders on the subject?

2. Is patriotism wrong? Is there some way patriotic Christians can become detached enough from the interests of their country to decide on their own whether a particular war is justified?

PART THREE

Why Some Christians Refuse to Fight

CHAPTER 8

Taking Jesus Seriously

The history of Christianity is strewn with the debris of countless wars. Over these battlefields is heard the wailing of widows, of orphans, of the maimed and blinded, and the moans of the wounded, the gassed, the pierced and battered. Here echo the blows, the explosions, and the shrill whistle of falling bombs.

In spite of this history, the Spirit of God has been quietly at work. God has preserved an oasis of peace. A people of peace. The learned doctors will forever discuss Cicero, Augustine, Thomas Aquinas, Martin Luther, Camilo Torres, and the rest. And mainstream Christianity will glibly sign up for the excitement and glamour of the next military parade into destruction. But somewhere, always, the Lord will have at least a few Christians who turn to the Scriptures for guidance. Men and women of courage who will not deny the teaching of Jesus in favor of other values.

They have not always been remembered by history. But God never forgets. To mention a few that we do know of: Peter Waldo and the early Waldensians, beginning in the twelfth century; Peter Chelcicky and the Czech Unity of Brethren, in the fifteenth century; Menno Simons and the Anabaptists, beginning in the sixteenth century; George Fox and the Society of Friends (Quakers), beginning in the seventeenth century; Martin Luther King and many others who have refused "justified" violence in the twentieth century. And the many, many martyrs, right down to our own generation, who have died rather than kill.

Something becomes immediately obvious when we observe the writings of these dissenters. Their arguments are pursued at another level, without an effort to sound reasonable in non-Christian terms. Just-war thinking sounds reasonable to Christians and non-Christians alike. Biblical pacifism requires conversion to make sense. It is intensely spiritual. It requires "the mind of Christ." The only way it is convincing is if the Holy Spirit convicts. In the words of Paul, "The man without the Spirit does not accept the things that come from the Spirit of God, for they are foolishness to him, and he cannot understand them, because they are spiritually discerned" (1 Corinthians 2:14, NIV).

If Jesus Really Matters

The case for biblical pacifism begins and ends with Jesus. It goes beyond the Sermon on the Mount; it is Jesus himself. It is incarnation. It is the Christian belief that Jesus fully reflected the nature of God. That Jesus is what people will be like if they bother to do God's will.

Biblical pacifists really do believe that Jesus is the complete, definitive revelation of God's will for humankind. They really do believe he is the eternal *Logos* of God, become flesh. That is, he is the eternal message of God—the Word—made visible in human history so God need never again be misunderstood. His life and example stand for us in many ways, but especially in the matter of relating to enemies.

Jesus too had enemies, you see. His nation had deeply hated enemies. His people were oppressed. They suffered great injustice at the hands of a political system which kept them in misery. According to Luke, his mother and her relative Zechariah both composed stirring poems before Jesus was born. In these they captured dramatically the affliction and deepest desires of their people. Surely Mary taught her child to long for the same things, to identify the same enemies!

So Jesus had national enemies. He also had political enemies and religious enemies. Perhaps some of them came to be personal enemies as well. So when Jesus holds up his own enemy-love as an example for his disciples, he is not off in a never-never unreal religious world where enemies don't matter. He is in a world where your country's enemies torture you to death on a cross.

Suppose Jesus had never said to turn the other cheek. Suppose he had never said we are to love those who hate us. Or that he had never said we are to forgive unconditionally. Even so, those who take him seriously would still be unable to fight. Because he taught us to love *as he loved*.

And the way he loved us, his enemies, was to die for our sins rather than punish us. He suffered our injustice against him rather than treat us with the justice we deserved. The apostles were aware that Jesus' death in favor of his enemies was meant as an example to be followed:

> Christ himself suffered for you and left you an example, so that you would follow in his steps. . . . When he was insulted, he did not answer back with an insult; when he suffered, he did not threaten, but placed his hopes in God, the righteous Judge. (1 Peter 2:21b, 23)

If God had intended his people to bear the injustice and sin of the world, *what could he have said or done beyond what he did in Jesus Christ?* If we will not understand it this way, how *would* we understand it?

What of the Old Testament?

Christians who refuse to fight have a variety of ways of dealing with warfare in the Old Testament. Some believe that what applied before God's final revelation in Christ is inferior to Christ himself. If and when the New Testament contradicts the Old Testament, the New is superior. This applies not only to war and enemy-love, it applies equally to the Sabbath, food laws, and so on. No explanation need be given for God's change of policy. It is his exclusive right as sovereign Lord.

Others blame human frailty and inability to understand God fully. God's will never really was the destruction of Israel's enemies. Because of the hardness of their hearts, however, he allowed it and even made provision for it.

There are other explanations biblical pacifists give. But in no case do they agree to use Old Testament warfare as a model for Christian behavior.

What of Romans 13:1-7?

In Romans 13:1-7, the apostle instructs Christians to submit to government authority. This is because God intends government to punish those who do evil and reward those who do good. Christians who refuse to fight, however, interpret this passage in a way radically different from Christians who go to war.

Some do not believe God positively commands government to use the sword. Rather, God has put order into the fact that people *will* use the sword, regardless. Sword-bearing government is the order God brings to humanity's sin. But it is still *sin* which requires it. It is not God's original purpose for human society.

Others would grant that government is required before God to use the sword when necessary. They hold that government would be sinfully irresponsible if it did not do so. Even so, nothing in the passage suggests that *Christians* should ever be in government.

Usually biblical pacifists point out that the context for this paragraph, beginning with chapter 12 and including what follows in chapter 13, clearly instructs Christians *not* to avenge evil. Therefore, the *Christian's* duty is clear enough, whatever anybody else's duties and rights might be.

A further argument along the same lines is that no one can serve two masters. One cannot follow Christ in private life, and follow the demands of an "office" the rest of the time. A Christian soldier must first of all be a Christian, if he or she is a Christian at all. The Christian is *always* bound to follow Christ in total enemy-love.

War is sin. It is sin for everyone. It is not God's will in any positive way that people kill each other. Now, people will kill each other anyway, of course. God in God's sovereignty often manages to turn this sin toward good results. That in no way justifies the sin. It merely shows God's greatness.

The Need for a New Birth

Biblical pacifists arrive at an absolute rejection of war through the Scriptures. Other Christians have arrived at similar convictions through other paths.

Some believe human society is constantly evolving in the direction of justice, equality, and understanding. Their optimism fails to take human sin into account. The result has been a shallow pacifism. This pacifism has not held up to the test when evil and sin cause a real war, and real human suffering gets out of hand.

For others, notably the Quakers (Society of Friends), the path toward pacifism has been an intense inner experience. The Spirit of Christ is the same today as 2,000 years ago. This Spirit reveals himself as an inner light to those who are open. Friends trust that if one is truly open to God, one will find it difficult, if not impossible, to kill another person. God within us creates in us a strong revulsion at even the thought of taking human life. For Friends this is enough. Even without the Bible, they would still need to follow this inner light.

Menno Simons lived a century before the Friends appeared on the scene of history. He was a Dutch Christian who believed it was possible in his own day to follow Jesus, even when the church at large was saying it was neither possible nor necessary. His position on war was what we have labeled *biblical* pacifism. Mennonites have traditionally called it non-resistance. But in Menno's insistence on *regeneration*, or new birth, the effect is similar to what Friends describe as the work of the inner light:

> The regenerate, therefore, lead a penitent and new life, for they are renewed in Christ and have received a new heart and spirit. Once they were earthly minded, now heavenly; once they were carnal, now spiritual; once they were unrighteous, now righteous; once they were evil, now good. . . . Hatred and vengeance they do not know for they love those who hate them; they do good to those who despitefully use them, and pray for those who persecute them.[20]

> I tell you the truth in Christ, the rightly baptized disciples of Christ, note well, they who are baptized inwardly with Spirit and fire, and externally with water, according to the Word of the Lord, have no weapons except patience, hope, silence, and God's Word. . . . And iron and metal spears and swords we leave to those who, alas, regard human blood and swine's blood about alike. He that is wise let him judge what I mean.[21]

Questions for Reflection and Discussion

1. If God *had* intended his people to bear the injustice and sin of the world rather than attempt to correct it or punish it themselves, *what could he have said or done beyond what he did in Jesus Christ?* If we will not understand it this way, how will we understand it (see p. 76)?

2. Read again Menno Simons' description of regenerate or born-again Christians. If you read carefully you will note that just about every phrase calls a Bible verse to mind. Does Menno's description describe the people you know who call themselves born-again? If it does not, do you believe Menno's description of "born-again-ness" is mistaken? (Please note the quotation is incomplete; Menno also mentioned *other* characteristics of born-again Christians.)

CHAPTER 9

Acting for a Shalom World

Justice—whether or not Christians should act for justice in the world—is not the point of disagreement. Christians who fight have often stated that they are interested in justice as well as love. But according to them, Christians who refuse to fight are interested only in love.

That is not so. Biblical pacifists will agree that the justice and love of God are inseparable. You cannot have one without the other.

The only argument is *how* you work for justice. Curiously, everybody agrees that justice is always one of the first victims in war. So Christian pacifists would argue that if the aim is justice, war is simply the wrong way to go after it. You cannot paint a wall white with black paint.

Peace: God's Alternative to War

Before going further, we must explain that strange foreign word in the title, *shalom* (rhymes with "the home"). Shalom is the biblical idea of peace, therefore an important concept.

You will recall that biblical pacifists refuse to kill because of the positive urge to love as Jesus loved. There is much more to this love than simply not to kill. Remember the parable of the good Samaritan? The love of Christ is a *positive* way to treat neighbors and enemies. Of course, that love has to include not killing them. But love is so much more than just not killing!

In the same way, the Bible does not have much to say against war. Some would argue it has nothing to say against war! Yet, it does have a well-developed message for *peace*. Now, this peace is not the absence of war or strife, as we often understand it. It is shalom. So, again, what is shalom?

Shalom is not something kings or rulers can achieve by keeping a nation out of war or by signing treaties. A nation can be free of international conflict and still not be at peace, biblically understood. *For this peace is the harmony, the total order which can come only when no one is suffering.* The suffering of any one segment of society destroys the peace, for it stands in the way of shalom. If anyone is oppressed, denied human dignity, or condemned to suffer want while others have an abundance, then there is no peace.

This peace, this shalom, is a mark of the kingdom of God. You remember how Jesus announced the kingdom, reading from Isaiah:

> The Spirit of the Lord is upon me,
> because he has chosen me
> to bring good news to the poor.
> He has sent me to proclaim liberty
>   to the captives

and recovery of sight to the blind,
to set free the oppressed
and announce that the time has come
when the Lord will save his people.

(Luke 4:18-19)

To say it another way, Jesus came to bring shalom. This is what the Jews were expecting from their messiah. But then he turned around and surprised them. This peace was not only an internal domestic policy, but extended to foreigners as well. In his parable of the Good Samaritan, Jesus showed that it is possible for both Jew and Samaritan to experience shalom. Jesus commissioned his disciples to proclaim the gospel of his kingdom. He foresaw that eventually this shalom would reach into the farthest corners of the earth.

Christians for a New Social Order

Since shalom is the nature of biblical peace, Christians who refuse to go to war are sometimes also at the forefront of liberation movements. The two do not always go together. We have already noticed how some Christians who are for liberation justify resorting to war to accomplish it. On the other hand, the fact that some Christians have rejected war does not necessarily mean they have caught a vision for biblical peace.

Let us observe how it works when pacifism and liberation do go together. We will need to begin with the phrase "nonviolent direct action."

Nonviolent direct action confronts society with the suffering imposed on certain people by the usual state of things. It makes visible the violence in society of which only the victims are usually aware —the suffering of the minorities, of the poor and powerless. Yet nonviolent direct action does not fight this "institutional violence" through terrorism or new violence.

Some years ago, many people who lived in Montgomery, Alabama, quit using the city's buses. They chose to walk instead of ride. Why did they take this "unnecessary" hardship upon themselves? Their action stood as a witness to the injustice of a system which gave white-skinned people special privileges. In certain parts of the United States, some seats on buses could not be used by people with black or brown skin. This arrangement was known as segregation. It affected every area of life, not just buses. Through this bus boycott in Montgomery and many other similar actions, segregation was eventually abolished in the United States.

Dom Helder Camara, a Brazilian Christian, is totally committed to the cause of justice in his country. He has stated that he understands those who choose terrorism and war in their effort to bring liberation and justice to Latin America. Yet concerning himself he says:

> I hereby give my person, physical and spiritual, to nonviolent action. Consequently, I am committed to keeping the following commandments:
>
> to meditate every day upon the preaching of Christ;
> to bear in mind that nonviolent action has reconciliation and justice as its end, rather than victory;

to keep in my conduct and in my words an attitude of
love, because God is love;

to pray every day and ask of God the grace to be his
instrument, so that all might become free;

to sacrifice my personal interests so that all might
become free;

to observe toward my enemies, as much as toward my
friends, the rules of courtesy;

to try to consecrate myself habitually to the service of
others and of the world;

to avoid violence, both the violence of the hands and
the violence of the tongue and heart . . . .[22]

One of the objectives of this approach is the conversion of enemies. Nonviolent direct action can at
times be very upsetting. It can have the appearance
of creating conflict rather than resolving it. Yet, it is
never aimed at destroying the enemy. It seeks out the
humanity, morality, and conscience that remain in
those who profit through the suffering of others.

Those who choose violence would rather dismiss
the enemy as evil beyond redemption. In this respect,
the attitude of those who passively accept injustice is
no different. They also believe the oppressor is evil
beyond redemption. But those who choose nonviolent
action believe no one is so evil that he or she cannot
be changed. Aware of their own dependence on the
grace of God, they become aware of the spiritual
need of their enemy. They would say something like,
"God's grace and love have changed my life and
understanding. I believe God can change you too!"

Yet nonviolence is the way of suffering and martyrdom. It has tremendous power to bring persons to

their moral senses. But the source of this power comes from people taking suffering upon themselves, rather than causing others to suffer.

Is This Just Another Pagan Influence?

We have stated at the outset—and observed at several points since—that most Christian understandings of war have their roots in pagan thought. It is impossible to talk of nonviolence without mentioning Gandhi, not himself a Christian. He used nonviolent means to win the independence of India from England.

Is the use of nonviolent direct action just another example of Christians reverting to pagan ideology instead of basing their beliefs and action on Jesus Christ? Perhaps.

Yet Gandhi openly acknowledged the influence of the life and thought of Jesus upon his beliefs and conduct. It is possible that this person who refused to call himself a Christian may have taken Christ more seriously than many Christians!

The relationship between Gandhi and nonviolent action is not one of Christians basing their behavior on non-Christian thought. It is rather a case of non-Christians basing their behavior, at least in part, upon Jesus Christ. No wonder many Christians see Jesus through new eyes after learning about Gandhi.

Seeking First the Kingdom of God

Many biblical pacifists feel uncomfortable with any tactic—violent or nonviolent—which seeks to force change upon society. They believe in an alternative way to work toward shalom in human society. It is to build among God's people a model of peaceful society.

Where men and women have not been born again, there is no chance of their living in genuine peace. Carnal men and women cannot live Spirit-filled relationships. Where the light of God does not shine, there is always darkness. Where Jesus is not allowed to reign as Lord, sin is always the dominant element in social relationships.

To admit this is to say that Christians are called to be "in" the world, but not "of" the world. They cannot take responsibility for a society which rejects their Lord. But they can take responsibility for living in justice and fairness among those who have been called to a new life in Jesus Christ. Although others refuse to hear the Word of God, biblical pacifists can still call *each other* to accountability.

Their way to build a shalom world, then, is to live today the way the whole world will live when Christ returns. To seek today the kingdom—that is, the actualized government—of God. To build the church in worship, love, joy, and justice. And then to invite others to join them through conversion. This conversion to Jesus Christ will mean a radical break with injustice and violence in any form.

Questions for Reflection and Discussion

1. Nonviolent direct action is not inherently a "Christian" method for bringing about justice. That is, people of many different kinds of beliefs engage in it. It often involves breaking laws which uphold justice.

How comfortable do you feel, as a Christian, with demonstrations, marches, boycotts, and other such activities? Is breaking the law always incompatible with the apostolic teaching on submission to authority? Do you believe people who are accustomed to using power oppressively are likely to change under the pressure of such activity? Can you think of a better way to work for change?

2. This book is one in a collection called the "Peace and Justice Series." Do you agree that peace and justice go together? If you are a concientious objector to military service, have you also engaged in activity on behalf of justice? If you are an activist for justice, are you persuaded that only nonviolent means are legitimate?

CHAPTER 10

Turning Our Backs on Christendom

At the end of the first chapter, we described the birth of Christendom. In the Christendom arrangement, Christians take responsibility for society. They run the government and decide when military force is necessary.

We now have 16 centuries of this arrangement to look back on. Christians took on this responsibility because they were convinced that if they ran things, a new age of peace, justice, and love would arrive. For this high ideal, they forsook the early teaching of Christianity concerning enemy-love. It is time Christians gave an account of how they have managed.

What we see certainly does not look good. We must answer for the way Christians of Europe and the United States have treated the native population on the American continent. We must answer for the horror of Christian European colonization in Africa, the enslavement of her native people, and the current injustice in South Africa.

We must answer for the manner in which Christians from Europe colonized the Far East, and our moral inferiority before Gandhi. We must answer for the centuries of anti-Semitic policies, the horror of persecution of Jews down to the Nazi Holocaust of our own age. We must answer for Hiroshima and Nagasaki. We must answer for 16 centuries of war, pillage, and rape while we were responsible for society. God forbid we should have to answer for the nuclear annihilation of all life on this planet!

Is it possible anything worse might have happened during these past 16 centuries if government and the sword had been left to pagans? Have Christians really achieved "lesser" evils, or about the same kind of evils that were to be expected anyhow? Honest, now.

In taking responsibility for government, for power and war, the church lost sight of its true mission. Christ knew better than to take the devil's offer of worldly power, but his church thought it could do better. The devil gave it authority. He gave it power. He gleefully gave it the "right" to end the lives of people God had created in God's own image. And the church paid for it with its soul.

In our own age, it is possible a post-Christendom generation has taken over in Europe. If this is so, things there will probably get no better. But at least Christians will no longer be to blame. Christians there might again be free to inspire hope instead of fear. In most of Africa and Asia, Christendom was never a real possibility. Christians there have usually been in the minority. But what of the Americas, North and South?

There are so many Christians who simply cannot imagine a world in which we do not take responsibility for all of society! So many Christians have never stopped to consider seriously whether the only way to make a relevant contribution to society is to be in control. And they have simply assumed that being willing to kill enemies is a reasonable price to pay for being in control. Many Christians have blindly believed the serpent's whisper that only through violence and warfare can justice and peace arrive.

We have a long way to go yet before Christians stand united again in practical love for enemies. A long way lies ahead before we turn again to God's shalom instead of the blood-soaked "peace" which weapons bring.

When War Is Justified, the Result Is Always War

Many Christians still think just-war thinking is basically sound. We just need to *apply* it consistently. Meaning, when wars are not just, Christians must say so clearly and refuse to fight. But what happens when they try to do this? They meet the same fate principled Christian pacifists have always met. Their position is labeled irrelevant, or worse, irresponsible. The world is happy to have a Christian opinion on wars as long as that Christian opinion justifies its wars. But when a Christian says we must not fight, it seems his or her opinion is not worthy to be heard.

Concerned Christians ever since Augustine have been trying to say that only certain wars are justified. What the world hears is that it is certainly possible to justify wars. What it means in practice is that Christians are certain to fight in wars and then to find a fitting justification for them.

This is how just-war thinking ever since Constantine and Augustine has worked. People simply go on killing each other as usual. And then the theologians follow behind and explain why it was necessary.

By refusing to say that all war is always sin, Christians who believe in just wars feed a monster and expect to control it. But they always lose control. Their ability to actually keep people from killing each other is no greater than if Christians always refused to kill on the basis of principle. I am inclined to think it is probably quite a bit less. If the idea of just-war thinking is to control or stop wars, wouldn't it be better simply for Christians to stop fighting? The slogan of the hippies in the United States in the 60s may actually hold some insight: "What if they held a war, and nobody came?"

Utopian? Of course it is. But is it any more so than to imagine Christians can end the suffering and injustice of the world by returning bullet for bullet and bomb for bomb?

Discovering What Action Really Matters

A common thread runs through the thought of all Christians who justify fighting. It is the belief that government, politics, warfare, police, and so on, carry the position of first importance in human affairs. This belief influences one's reading of history and one's understanding of human affairs in general. One begins to view life as a matter of violent people and institutions savagely competing with each other. This is what is really significant.

But if this belief is true, then Jesus must be

irrelevant in human affairs, as in fact we have seen he *is* to many Christians. But Jesus tried to make the opposite truth clear. Jesus himself attributed ultimate significance to his ministry of healing and teaching. This is why he was neither a Zealot (Jewish revolutionary) nor a centurion (Roman military officer), nor a Constantine-style emperor. He considered those other types of action in society not nearly as significant.

Where does significant change occur today in our world? Is it in the courts of power, as Constantine, Augustine, and defenders of "justifiable" wars would have us believe? Or is it in the quiet faithfulness of the true followers of Jesus in all his meekness?

Origen, who wrote before Christians embraced warfare, believed the latter was true. He said the prayers of Christians are better at bringing peace and justice to society than all the emperor's soldiers.

How is wickedness really restrained? By the might of rulers or by the spiritual authority of the prayers of God's people? Or do Christians no longer believe in the power of prayer?

I have before me an article from *El Pais*, one of the major newspapers in Spain. It displays a large photo of a *yogi* levitating about a foot off the ground. The article is about Transcendental Meditation (TM), those who practice it, and the claims they make.

> Where one percent of the population do TM, the stress of society is neutralized and, for instance, crime decreases. They go even farther. They claim that world peace could be achieved by the same means.

To explain it they resort to the theory of the unified field. . . .[23]

It sounds like so much nonsense to me. But I admire their faith. They believe there is more to the problem of war than meets the eye. That there are hidden powers in the universe which affect human society. They believe there are solutions other than just to take part in the killing. Christians used to talk like that too.

Finally, build up your strength in union with the Lord and by means of his mighty power. Put on all the armor that God gives you, so that you will be able to stand up against the Devil's evil tricks. For we are not fighting against human beings but against the wicked spiritual forces in the heavenly world, the rulers, authorities, and cosmic powers of this dark age. So put on God's armor now! Then when the evil day comes, you will be able to resist the enemy's attacks; and after fighting to the end, you will still hold your ground. . . . Do all this in prayer, asking for God's help. Pray on every occasion, as the Spirit leads.

(Ephesians 6:10-13, 18a)

Fighting the Real Enemy

Christians who justify war think they have the perfect example in World War II. Hitler was so terrible, so utterly evil, only military force could stop him.

But they have mistaken the enemy. Hitler was only flesh and blood. They have fallen for the age-old mistake of believing that the battle against evil is against flesh and blood rather than against the dark spiritual forces of the universe.

Hitler was killed, but his ideas had been bred by the spirit of a violent civilization which many today have also embraced. At Hitler's death, this spirit didn't just disappear, of course. It has lived on in other self-righteous causes, many of which were already being shaped even before Hitler came to power. The sheer amount of death and suffering caused by each of these other fanaticisms may not match the Holocaust, but the underlying self-justification and intolerance is certainly every bit as evil and selfish.

This is what lies behind the conflicts which sadden our present generation: Israelis and Palestinians, Soviets in Eastern Europe and Afghanistan, United States' policy in Central America and Vietnam, fundamentalist zealots in Iran, Idi Amin and Milton Obote in Uganda, apartheid in South Africa, the circumstance of *desaparecidos* in Argentina and Central America, "cultural revolution" in China, Pinochet in Chile, Pol Pot in Cambodia. The spirit of Hitler has multiplied and lives on.

The Bible shows how Canaanite and Philistine values in the end conquered the Israelites who had set out to exterminate them through idealistic warfare. This was a hard and humbling lesson that the prophets were finally able to admit. At least they confessed the effect, though they themselves never traced matters to this fundamental problem arising from the origins of Israel. In a similar way, the oppressive spirit of czarism conquered the Bolsheviks who had set out to free the Russian people.

Certainly Hitler had to be stopped. But how? Did

everyone else have to become as smugly self-right-eous as he about their ideals, and as willing to destroy those who stood in their way? Oh, the wicked unbelief of those who refuse to understand that Christ had already conquered Hitler on the cross centuries ago!

Certainly in the real world where naive idealism is dangerous fantasy, Hitler had to be stopped. But as Christians, we believe the real world includes demonic forces which drive people to such extreme wickedness. If this is so, to kill a wicked man may be far more foolish than so-called realists had ever imagined.

Jesus, the apostles, and early Christianity knew this once. They consistently resisted the devil. James wrote, "Submit yourselves to God. Resist the devil, and he will run away from you" (James 4:7). As promised, the devil fled when they resisted him. But a fundamental element of the resistance was to not be drawn into the trap of destroying the people he used. Such people were only his bait, and very much his victims. No, they were never sidetracked by this monstrous temptation. It was the devil himself they resisted.

As we resist evil—and the evil one—in our own day, will we prove as wise as the saints of old? Will we be able to keep our minds clear and our hearts pure?

A clear answer must now be given to the question, "Why do Christians make war?" Because they have found fighting the devil by spiritual means to be too big a challenge—too scary and faith-demanding. It is much less complicated simply to kill people!

Why do some Christians still make peace after the manner of Jesus? Because his defenseless death on behalf of us, who were his enemies, is still capable of inspiring us to follow in his steps. And because we take his resurrection to be convincing proof of the power of God to destroy strongholds of unrighteousness if we will only believe.

Questions for Reflection and Discussion

1. Is it possible anything worse might have happened during the past 16 centuries if government and sword had been left to pagans? Have Christians really achieved "lesser" evils, or about the same kinds of evils that were to be expected anyway (see p. 90)?

2. Do you believe there are spiritual forces behind good and evil in human society? Are human beings ever the real enemy, to the extent that killing them is the only realistic solution? Do you believe that prayer can accomplish anything if it is not accompanied by vigorous Christian use of *human* power and authority as well?

Notes

1. Cicero, *De Oficiis*, xi, in Arthur F. Holmes, *War and Christian Ethics* (Grand Rapids: Baker Books, 1975), pp. 28f.

2. Augustine, *Epist.*, 189, 6, in Holmes, ibid., pp. 62f.

3. Augustine, *On the Free Will*, I, 4, 9; I, 5, 12, in Jean-Michel Hornus, *It Is Not Lawful for Me to Fight* (Scottdale: Herald Press, 1980), p. 181.

4. Augustine, *Epist.*, 138, ii, 14; *Sermo Dom.*, 1, xx, 63, 70; *Epist.*, 138, ii,15, in Roland H. Bainton, *Christian Attitudes Toward War and Peace* (Nashville: Abingdon Press, 1960), p. 97.

5. Nestarius of Calama. Augustine, *Epist.*, 103, 4, in W. H. C. Frend, *The Donatist Church* (Oxford: Clarendon Press, 1952), p. 239.

6. Luther, Letter to John Ruhel, May 23, 1525, from Clyde Manschreck, ed., *A History of Christianity*, Vol. II (Englewood Cliffs: Prentice-Hall, 1964), p. 38.

7. Thomas Aquinas, *Summa Theologica* 2-2, Q. 42, Art. 2, in Holmes, op. cit., p. 117.

8. John Locke, *Second Treatise on Civil Government*, chap. 19 (232), Holmes, ibid., p. 269.

9. Camilo Torres, as quoted by Feliciano Blazquez, *Persona, Revolución y Violencia* (Salamanca: Sigueme, 1975), p. 202. (My translation.)

10. Gustavo Gutierrez, *Teología de la Liberación* (Salamanca: Sigueme, 1985), p. 357. (My translation.)

11. Pope Urban II, as quoted in William R. Durland, *No King but Caesar?* (Scottdale: Herald Press, 1975), p. 96.

12. Jacques Ellul, *The Subversion of Christianity* (Grand Rapids: Eerdmans, 1986), pp. 102f.

13. Julia Ward Howe, stanzas three and four, as printed in *The Golden Book Of Favorite Songs* (Minneapolis: Shmitt, Hall & McCreary, 1951), p. 12.

14. Ernesto Cardenal, *El Evangelio en Solentiname, II* (Salamanca: Sigueme, 1978), pp. 136f. (My translation.)

15. As quoted in Bainton, op. cit., p. 110.

16. Erasmus, "On Beginning War," *The Education of a Christian Prince*, in Holmes, op. cit., p. 180.

17. Arthur F. Holmes, "A Just War: Defining Some Key Issues," in Oliver R. Barclay, ed., *Pacifism and War* (Leicester: InterVarsity, 1984), p. 31.

18. Ibid., p. 32.

19. Mark Twain, *The Adventures of Huckleberry Finn* (New York: Signet, 1959), p. 111.

20. Menno Simons, *The Complete Writings* (Scottdale: Herald Press, 1956), p. 93.

21. Ibid., p. 198.

22. Helder Camara, from *La Revolución de los No-Violentos*, as quoted in Blazquez, op. cit., pp. 223f.

23. *El Pais* (Madrid), March 22, 1987, "Domingo," p. 22.

For Further Reading

Bainton, Roland H. *Christian Attitudes Toward War and Peace*. Nashville, Tennessee: Abingdon, 1960, 299 pages. This is the standard classic historical introduction to the subject. Very readable.

Barclay, Oliver R., ed. *Pacifism and War*. Leicester, England: InterVarsity, 1984, 256 pages. Eight prominent Christians debate a series of theses on the subject. Not light reading, but a good articulation of a variety of positions.

Clouse, Robert G., ed. *War: Four Christian Views*. Downers Grove, Illinois: InterVarsity, 1981, 210 pages. Four Christian authors debate the issue, defending biblical nonresistance, Christian pacifism, just war, and preventive war positions. Very readable.

Durland, William R. *No King But Caesar?* Scottdale, Pennsylvania: Herald Press, 1975, 182 pages. A survey of biblical issues and church history which comes out in favor of pacifism.

Holmes, Arthur F., ed. *War and Christian Ethics*. Grand Rapids, Michigan: Baker, 1975, 356 pages. A collection of source readings covering all historical periods and a great variety of positions. For those who want it straight from the original thinkers. Serious reading.

Peachey, Paul, ed. *Peace, Politics, and the People of God.* Philadelphia, Pennsylvania: Fortress, 1986, 184 pages. The ecumenical dialogue on war/ peace issues in the past 20 years. Serious reading.

Wenger, J. C. *The Way of Peace.* Scottdale, Pennsylvania: Herald Press, 1977, 72 pages. A brief survey of Christ's teachings on love and of the way of peace through the centuries. Easy reading.

Yoder, John H. *Christian Attitudes to War, Peace, and Revolution.* Elkhart, Indiana: Goshen Biblical Seminary, 1983, 602 pages. The most complete study available on the subject from a noted Mennonite scholar. Serious reading.

_____. *Nevertheless: The Varieties of Religious Pacifism.* Scottdale, Pennsylvania: Herald Press, 1971, 142 pages. Clear descriptions of 16 different ways to be against war.

_____. *What Would You Do?* Scottdale, Pennsylvania: Herald Press, 1983, 136 pages. Answers to the age-old question, "What would you do if someone was attacking your mother, sister, girlfriend?" Includes a variety of real-life stories.

The Author

Dennis Byler was born in Bragado, Argentina. His parents were Mennonite missionaries in Argentina and Uruguay.

He served for a number of years on the pastoral team of the Bragado Mennonite Church, and was active with youth ministries at the national level for Mennonites in Argentina. He also served with Mennonite Board of Missions for a year as an itinerant Bible teacher with the Tobas of northern Argentina.

He is married to Connie Bentson. They have a son and three daughters, born between 1975 and 1986. Two of their children were born in Argentina, another in the United States, and the fourth in Spain.

Dennis and Connie are members of Fellowship of Hope Mennonite Church, Elkhart, Indiana. At the time they joined it was an intentional Christian community. Since 1981 they have been serving in Burgos, Spain, under joint sponsorship of the Shalom Covenant Communities and Mennonite Board of Missions.

In Burgos, Dennis has done a variety of things at

different times. These include support and counsel for a Christian community with a ministry of rehabilitation for drug addicts; pastoral counseling and preaching; as well as Bible teaching, leadership training, and extensive writing— mostly in Spanish. (In Spanish, he signs his writing as Dionisio Byler.)

Dennis/Dionisio is a graduate of Goshen College, and holds an M.Div. degree from Goshen Biblical Seminary.

PEACE AND JUSTICE SERIES

Edited by J. Allen Brubaker and Elizabeth Showalter

This series of books sets forth briefly and simply some important emphases of the Bible concerning war and peace and how to deal with conflict and injustice. The authors write from within the Anabaptist tradition. This includes viewing the Scriptures as a whole as the believing community discerns God's Word through the guidance of the Spirit.

Some of the titles reflect biblical, theological, or historical content. Other books in the series show how these principles and insights are practical in daily life.

The books in this series are published in North America by:

Herald Press
616 Walnut Avenue
Scottdale, PA 15683
USA

Herald Press
117 King Street, West
Kitchener, ON N2G 4M5
CANADA

Persons wanting copies for distribution overseas or permission to translate should write to the Scottdale address listed above.